Cornerstones of Freedom

John Brown's Raid on Harpers Ferry

BRENDAN JANUARY

CHILDREN'S PRESS®
A Division of Grolier Publishing
New York • London • Hong Kong • Sydney
Danbury, Connecticut

Visit Children's Press on the Internet at:
http://publishing.grolier.com

Library of Congress Cataloging-in-Publication Data

January, Brendan, 1972–
    John Brown's raid on Harpers Ferry / Brendan January.
    p. cm.— (Cornerstones of freedom)
Includes index.
    Summary: Recounts the story of John Brown's failed rebellion in Harpers
Ferry in 1859, intended to start a massive slave uprising in the South and the
establishment of a state in the Allegheny Mountains for freed slaves.
    ISBN: 0-516-21144-7 (lib. bdg.) 0-516-27037-0 (pbk.)
    1. Harpers Ferry (W. Va.)—History—John Brown's Raid, 1859 Juvenile
literature. 2. Brown, John, 1800–1859 Juvenile literature. [1. Harpers Ferry
(W. Va.)—History—John Brown's Raid, 1859. 2. Brown, John, 1800–1859.
3. Abolitionists.] I. Title.
E451.J36 2000
973.7`116—dc21
                                            99-14965
                                            CIP

When John Brown was born in 1800, the United States was a young and growing country. Settlers poured into the new territories of the West. They built towns and turned forests into farmland. New states were added to the Union, and the country's population swelled. Americans were very proud of their country. Many people claimed there was more freedom in the United States than in any other country in the world. However, in the southern states, almost one million blacks wore the chains of slavery.

John Brown

In the early 1800s, most Americans were not concerned about slavery or the rights of black people. But John Brown's father was not like most Americans. He took the words of the Declaration of Independence, "all men are created equal," seriously. He taught his young son to respect all people and to consider slavery a sin against God. In addition to his father's teachings, John had other reasons to hate slavery. When he was only twelve years old, John watched in shock as a man beat a slave boy with an iron shovel. The terrible scene outraged young John and he was haunted by it as he grew older. At a crowded antislavery meeting in 1837, Brown rose from his seat and declared that he would spend the rest of his life trying to destroy slavery.

In the 1830s, only a small number of Americans agreed with Brown's view of slavery. These people, called abolitionists, argued that slavery was cruel and immoral. Southern slave owners reacted furiously to the abolitionists' criticism. They claimed that their slaves were happy and content. After spending a day in the field, slaves were guaranteed a meal and a place to sleep. That was more than many workers in northern states could expect.

But to most slaves, daily life was neither pleasant nor easy. One slave wrote, "No day ever dawns for the slave. . . . it is all night—all night forever." Another slave woman remembered, "Them days were hell. Babies was snatched

During the early 1800s, many northern antislavery societies formed to voice their support for the abolition of slavery.

4

Slaves worked from dawn to dusk on southern plantations and slave owners insisted the slaves were happy and well treated.

from their mothers and sold. . . . Children were separated from sisters and brothers and never saw each other again."

The breaking up of slave families infuriated Brown. Through the 1830s and 1840s, he helped escaped slaves flee north. He also met with black leaders and eagerly discussed plans to end slavery. Frederick Douglass, one of the best-known leaders of that time, said of Brown: "I have talked with many men, but I remember none who seemed so deeply excited upon the subject of slavery as he."

Frederick Douglass

In 1849, Brown moved his family to North Elba, a small community in the mountains of northern New York. There he devised a plan to destroy slavery once and for all. Brown's farm was located at the northern end of a mountain chain that stretched all the way south to Georgia. Rugged and covered with thick forests, the mountains provided excellent cover and plenty of places to hide. Some of these mountains, the Alleghenies, covered parts of the slave states of Virginia and Maryland. Brown believed that groups of armed men could ride out of the Alleghenies and attack nearby plantations. Moving at great speed, they could free hundreds of slaves and disappear into the mountains before the slave owners could fight back.

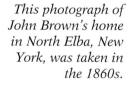

This photograph of John Brown's home in North Elba, New York, was taken in the 1860s.

Brown dreamed of establishing a new state in the Alleghenies where the slaves would be free. Former slaves would build churches, towns, and schools. They would own farms and plant crops. Brown did not fear attacks from the U.S. Army. In the narrow mountain passes, a handful of men could hold off thousands of soldiers. Brown imagined that as time passed, more and more slaves would flee the South and join him. Within a few years, the slave owners would be forced to abandon slavery.

John Brown planned to use the mountains as a highway to smuggle escaped slaves North. He also hoped to establish a free state in the Allegheny Mountains for former slaves.

MAINE

MINNESOTA

WISCONSIN

VT

NH

NORTH ELBA

NEW YORK

MASS.

CONN. RHODE ISLAND

MICHIGAN

PENNSYLVANIA

NEW JERSEY

IOWA

OHIO

DELAWARE MARYLAND

KANSAS-NEBRASKA TERRITORY

Opened to slavery in 1854

ILLINOIS

INDIANA

HARPERS FERRY

WASHINGTON DC

VIRGINIA

MISSOURI

KENTUCKY

NORTH CAROLINA

INDIAN TERRITORY

TENNESSEE

ARKANSAS

SOUTH CAROLINA

MISSISSIPPI

ALABAMA

GEORGIA

TEXAS

LOUISIANA

FLORIDA

Allegheny Mountains

mountain chain

free states

slave states

N

500 MILES

0   500 KM

While Brown made plans, the debate over slavery began to tear the nation apart. In 1854, the U.S. Congress passed a bill that opened a huge area of unsettled land—the Kansas-Nebraska Territory—to slavery. This bill shocked people in the North. They thought that Kansas would be reserved for farmers who didn't own slaves. Southerners were delighted because slavery would expand into the newly settled area.

In 1855, northerners and southerners rushed into Kansas. The proslavery groups hoped to pass laws that would establish slavery. The northerners, called "free-staters," wanted to keep the land for free farmers. In 1855, Brown traveled to Kansas with a wagon full of rifles and joined five of his sons, who were already with the free-state forces. Bitter fighting broke out between free-staters and those who supported slavery. Farms were burned, animals were stolen, and men were killed. On May 22, 1856, a proslavery army sacked and burned the city of Lawrence, Kansas. Two days later, a vengeful John Brown and several companions surprised five proslavery men as they slept in their cabins. Wielding giant knives, Brown and his companions stabbed them to death. The U.S. government immediately issued orders for Brown's arrest. But Brown kept fighting and won several small battles. Brown vowed, "I will die fighting for this cause. There will be no peace in this land until slavery is done for."

In early 1857, Brown left Kansas to travel east. In Connecticut, New York, and Massachusetts, he met with several admiring abolitionists. They pledged money and support to his cause. A small group of supporters, known as the Secret Six, were especially interested in Brown's daring plan to invade the South. They encouraged Brown to go forward with his plot. In spring 1858, Brown and several followers traveled to Chatham, Canada. There, Brown wrote a constitution and a plan of government for his free state in the Alleghenies. Brown had already selected the perfect target for attack—Harpers Ferry, Virginia.

This view of Harpers Ferry, Virginia, was photographed in 1859, around the time of Brown's raid.

Harpers Ferry was a small town built where two mighty rivers—the Shenandoah and the Potomac—meet. In 1859, only three thousand people lived in or around the town. But Brown was not interested in the people of Harpers Ferry. He was interested in the United States Armory and Arsenal at Harpers Ferry, which produced about ten thousand guns every year. By seizing the armory, Brown hoped to start a slave rebellion. News of Brown's attack would spread through the slave population. Thousands of slaves would flock to Harpers Ferry, where Brown would arm them with rifles. For those slaves who could not shoot a rifle, Brown would provide razor-sharp spears, known as pikes. Brown would then lead a mighty slave army south to free all the slaves and destroy slavery forever.

The engine house at Harpers Ferry, which Brown used during the raid, was later painted to read "John Brown's Fort" to attract the attention of train passengers traveling through town.

On July 3, 1859, Brown arrived in Harpers Ferry with two of his sons and one companion. Quietly, he rented a small farmhouse about 7 miles (11 kilometers) northeast of the town. This structure became Brown's head-quarters. In the following weeks, men and supplies arrived. Brown had met most of the men while fighting in Kansas. He ordered them to prepare for the raid. In a letter to his mother, one of Brown's men wrote, "I am now in a southern slave state, and before I leave it, it will be a free state, and so will every other one in the South."

A present-day view of Kennedy Farmhouse, located in Maryland near Harpers Ferry, that Brown used as a headquarters

In preparation for the attack, Brown studied maps of the South. He carefully wrote down the slave populations in each southern county. He had hoped the attack at Harpers Ferry would cause the entire slave population to revolt. But even if the attack failed, Brown reasoned, it could force the North and South into civil war. That war could strike a deathblow to slavery.

The men grew restless as the days passed. To keep the raid secret, Brown had forbidden them to leave the farmhouse. When visitors stopped by, the men were forced to hide in a cramped attic. Brown urged them to be patient. He hoped to receive more supplies from the North before ordering the men to attack.

Late in September, 950 pikes arrived and were added to a pile of 200 pistols and 198 rifles. Everything was almost ready. Finally, on October 15, 1859, Brown announced to his men that the attack would begin the next day.

On the evening of October 16, the men checked their weapons. Outside in the inky darkness, a light drizzle was falling. At 8 P.M., Brown gave the order: "Men, get your arms, we will proceed to the Ferry." Leaving three men to guard the farmhouse, the group formed two columns. Brown climbed into a wagon loaded with weapons and urged the horse onward. Eighteen men—five of them black and thirteen white—followed. The tiny "army" marched

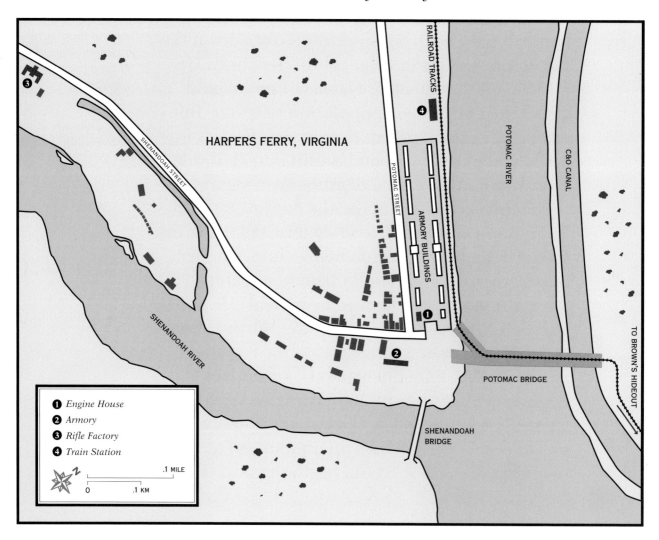

HARPERS FERRY, VIRGINIA

RAILROAD TRACKS

POTOMAC RIVER

C&O CANAL

SHENANDOAH STREET

POTOMAC STREET

ARMORY BUILDINGS

TO BROWN'S HIDEOUT

SHENANDOAH RIVER

POTOMAC BRIDGE

SHENANDOAH BRIDGE

❶ Engine House
❷ Armory
❸ Rifle Factory
❹ Train Station

.1 MILE
0   .1 KM

silently. The final struggle against slavery was about to begin.

The people of Harpers Ferry slept peacefully as John Brown and his band approached. As they neared the town, two men left the group to cut telegraph wires. The rest of the men continued on and soon arrived at the north end of the Potomac Bridge, a wooden covered bridge leading into Harpers Ferry. Brown swiveled in his wagon seat and gave a signal. Suddenly, two of Brown's men hurried across the bridge and captured the night watchman on the other side. With the bridge clear, the rest of the group joined them. Quickly they darted through the streets and surprised the watchman at the armory. "I come here from Kansas," Brown exclaimed to the shocked watchman, "and this is a slave state. I have possession of the United States Armory, and if the citizens interfere with me I must only burn the town and have blood!"

Brown's group then spread out into the town, capturing prisoners and putting them in a small engine house near the armory gate. Within minutes, Brown's group had seized the rifle factory. Everything was going according to Brown's plan. Soon, news of the revolt would spread like wildfire through Virginia and the rest of the South. Brown expected thousands of slaves to gather at Harpers Ferry, eager to join the war against slavery.

Meanwhile, a small group of Brown's men rode into the Virginia countryside. Their mission was to capture Colonel Lewis W. Washington, the great-grandnephew of President George Washington. Colonel Washington's plantation was only a few miles from Harpers Ferry. Under the cover of darkness, they stole into Washington's house and took him prisoner.

Quickly, the raiders placed him and his freed slaves in the wagon and rode back toward Harpers Ferry. They brought along one other item—a sword that

Colonel Lewis W. Washington

George Washington himself had owned. Brown wore the sword throughout the rest of the raid.

Back in Harpers Ferry, however, events were spinning out of Brown's control. At 1:30 A.M., a passenger-filled train came puffing into Harpers Ferry on its way to cross the Potomac Bridge. Brown's men blocked the train. Hayward Shepherd, a free black baggage handler, watched in confusion as the train stopped. He left his post to find out what was wrong. As he approached the bridge, Brown's men screamed at him to halt. Shepherd panicked and fled. Suddenly, one of the raiders fired his gun. The bullet knocked Shepherd to the ground. The night watchman dragged him to the train station, where he died several hours later. Ironically, the first man shot in John Brown's raid was a free black man.

By then, the crack of gunshots and urgent cries had awakened several people in Harpers Ferry. They stumbled from their beds in alarm and poured into the streets. As they wondered what was happening, rumors flew. Someone said it was a slave rebellion. Panic spread through the townspeople. Frantically, the men gathered rifles, pistols, and any weapon they could find. Down in town, a single churchbell began ringing. Its rhythmic sound carried an urgent message as it echoed across the countryside: Slave rebellion! Slave rebellion!

In the mist of the early morning, riders galloped into nearby towns shouting the news. Rebellion in Harpers Ferry! Men emptied out of their houses and began forming militia units. Within hours, the roads to Harpers Ferry were filled with nervous and excited men eager to stop Brown's rebellion.

Back in Harpers Ferry, Brown was unaware of the forces gathering to crush him. He allowed the passenger train to cross the bridge and

Troops and supplies cross the Potomac toward Harpers Ferry to put an end to John Brown's raid.

continue on. This proved to be a grave mistake. The conductor stopped at Monocacy, Maryland, and sounded the alarm. Telegraph wires began to hum, carrying the news to Washington, D.C., New York, Chicago, and across the nation: Slave rebellion in Harpers Ferry! In Washington, D.C., President James Buchanan was told of the crisis. He immediately ordered Colonel Robert E. Lee to take command of ninety U.S. Marines and hurry to Harpers Ferry.

Meanwhile in Harpers Ferry, armed men gathered along the hills and cliffs that surrounded the town. Brown was stunned by how quickly forces had assembled to fight him. He couldn't decide what to do next. One of Brown's party later recalled: "Captain Brown was all activity, though at times he was somewhat puzzled." Unwisely, Brown had scattered his tiny force. Some men remained in the rifle factory along the Shenandoah River. Others had returned to the farm for more supplies.

John Kagi, Brown's second in command, waited restlessly in the rifle factory. He sent a frantic note to Brown. "We must move immediately," he wrote. But Brown did not give the order. Brown received another note from Kagi, pleading that their tiny force gather and retreat. Again, Brown refused to budge. He expected a wagon filled with supplies to arrive from the farm at any moment.

President James Buchanan (top) and Colonel Robert E. Lee (bottom)

John Kagi

The supplies never arrived. Instead, a unit of militia from Charlestown arrived on the north end of the Potomac Bridge. Shooting their guns wildly, they dashed across the bridge. Brown, waving George Washington's sword, told his men: "The troops on the bridge are coming into the town. We will give them a warm reception." The militia rushed at Brown's position. Brown cried: "Let go upon them!"

Brown's men obeyed, firing volleys into the charging militia. Through the smoke, dust, and cries of the wounded, the militia retreated in confusion. But the brief battle cost Brown. One of his men, Dangerfield Newby, lay dead in the street, shot in the throat. An angry crowd of townspeople gathered around his body and began beating it with sticks.

Several dozen townsmen and farmers entered Harpers Ferry to join the fight against Brown. They broke into the saloons, drank heavily, and began shooting at everything that moved. The battle raged through the town. Hundreds of militia and farmers occupied the buildings and fences around the armory. Brown gathered the prisoners and the rest of his group into the small engine house on the armory grounds. Hastily, they barred the doors and began cutting rifle holes into the walls.

Brown realized that he was trapped. He sent his own son, Watson, and Aaron Stevens to

Dangerfield Newby, a former slave and the first of Brown's group to be killed, hoped the raid would allow him to free his wife and children, who were slaves on a Virginia plantation.

discuss a truce. Despite carrying a white flag, the symbol of surrender, both men were shot. Stevens fell bleeding into a gutter while Watson, gasping with pain, struggled back into the engine house. One of the prisoners carried Stevens to the train station.

Events began to turn rapidly against Brown and his men. Kagi and two men were surrounded and overrun at the rifle factory. Kagi escaped but was riddled with bullets as he desperately tried to swim across the Shenandoah River. The two men who were with him, John Copeland and Lewis Leary, fared little better. Leary fell mortally wounded while Copeland was taken prisoner.

John Copeland, a black college student, was captured while fighting with Kagi and Leary.

Brown sent out another note. He offered to trade his hostages for free passage across the Potomac River. But the militia had no intention of letting Brown escape. Instead, they increased their gunfire. Thousands of bullets smashed into the walls and doors of the engine house. Desperately, Brown and his men returned the shots. The battle continued on and off for hours. Several townspeople were hit in the crossfire, including the mayor of Harpers Ferry.

Will Thompson was twenty-six years old when he was killed at Harpers Ferry.

Brown then sent Will Thompson outside with another white flag. An angry mob seized Thompson and took him prisoner. "You may take my life," he cried. "Eighty thousand will arise to avenge me and carry out my purpose of giving liberty to the slaves." Enraged, the mob shot him and threw his body into the Potomac River.

As night fell, Brown paced restlessly in the cramped engine house. He was surrounded and cut off from escape. Few slaves had joined his rebellion. Two of his sons, Watson and Oliver, had been seriously wounded. Another of his group lay dead, killed by gunfire. Only four of his men remained unwounded. Eleven terrified prisoners huddled in a corner. Brown turned to them and spoke, "Gentlemen, if you knew of my past history you would not blame me for being here." Brown described to them his experiences in Kansas. Suddenly Brown turned and called out to Oliver.

Oliver Brown

There was no answer. "I guess he is dead . . . This is the third son I have lost in this cause."

At the first signs of daybreak, Brown and his exhausted men loaded their rifles and prepared for more battle. Outside in the armory yard stood Robert E. Lee and a unit of marines. Armed with rifles, bayonets, and sledgehammers, the marines prepared to storm the engine house. Behind them, thousands of people crowded the rooftops and streets of Harpers Ferry to watch.

Lee's second in command, Lieutenant J.E.B. Stuart, walked up to the engine house and knocked on the door. Brown cracked it open and pointed a rifle at Stuart's face. Stuart calmly gave Brown a note from Lee that demanded Brown's surrender. After a short conversation, Brown read the note and returned it to Stuart. "I prefer to die here," he said.

Watson Brown

Lieutenant J.E.B. Stuart led the attack on the engine house where Brown was hiding.

21

The marines stormed the engine house after Brown refused to surrender.

Stuart then jumped from the doorway and waved his hat as a signal to attack. With the crowds cheering behind them, the marines charged the engine house. Brown and his men poked their rifles through the gun-holes and began firing. But the marines could not be stopped. Using a heavy ladder as a battering ram, they broke down the door and burst inside. One marine was killed. Two of Brown's men were bayoneted. Brown was beaten unconscious and taken prisoner.

Only thirty-six hours old, Brown's war to free the slaves was over. Ten of Brown's men were dead or would die later from their wounds. Six of them were prisoners or would be captured later. Only five of Brown's men were able to escape.

Despite Brown's capture, the South remained in a state of panic for several days. Reports of slave rebellions spread from one town to the next. Armed groups of men nervously patrolled roads and bridges. The Baltimore *American and*

Commercial Advertiser reported: "The intelligence from Harpers Ferry has created an excitement in our community and throughout . . . the country that has scarcely been equalled."

Brown was placed under heavy guard. The next morning, officers, politicians, and reporters crowded into Brown's room. Everyone wanted an explanation for the raid. Despite his painful wounds, Brown answered their questions. One man demanded a reason for the attack. Brown turned to him: "I think, my friend, that you are guilty of a great wrong against God and humanity . . . and it would be right . . . to free those you willfully and wickedly hold in bondage." The session continued for several hours. Near the end of the meeting, Brown said: "I wish to say . . . that you had better, all you people of the South, prepare yourselves for a settlement of this question. . . . the negro question I mean; the end of that is not yet."

Newspapers throughout the country carried news of John Brown's raid. This portrait of Brown shows the beard he grew as a disguise to wear during the raid.

Brown and four of his captured men were moved to nearby Charlestown and ordered to stand trial. The entire country paid close attention. In the South, Brown's raid was labeled "an act of war." Few southerners believed that Brown had acted alone. They claimed that he was part of a bloody abolitionist plot to destroy slavery and the South. The Mobile [Alabama] *Register* stated: "For the first time the soil of the South has been invaded and its blood shed upon its own soil by armed abolitionists." Southerners' fears were encouraged by the

John Brown's trial, which took place in October 1859, was held in Charlestown, Virginia. (Brown is lying on the cot.)

discovery of Brown's papers at the farmhouse. They included letters from several northern abolitionists and maps of the South.

These letters and maps were presented at Brown's trial, which began on October 27, 1859. For three days, the lawyers argued and interviewed witnesses. The trial moved quickly. On October 31, Brown was found guilty of treason against the State of Virginia, conspiring with slaves, and murder. On November 2, Brown returned to the court to be sentenced. In the packed courtroom, Brown was asked if he had any words to say. Brown declared that he did. He stood and began to speak. For several minutes, Brown discussed the raid. He then described how the Bible "teaches me that all things . . . that men should do to me, I should do to them." This statement summarized Brown's belief. He wanted a world without slaves because it violated the words of the Bible and the will of God. He finished his speech by stating that he would gladly die for the slaves: "I say, let it be done." The judge sentenced Brown to hang on December 2.

Brown's words thrilled abolitionists in the North. One of Brown's supporters called the speech "unequalled in the history of American oratory for simplicity and power." Back in his cell, Brown was soon receiving dozens of visitors every day.

Most northerners, however, still regarded Brown with disgust and anger. They believed that the raid was wrong and that Brown should be punished. One northerner wrote: "The old idiot—the quicker they hang him and get him out of the way the better." But Brown wrote powerful and emotional letters that explained his actions and his hatred of slavery. They appeared in newspapers throughout the North. Brown's jailer, who had to read Brown's letters before sending them on, frequently wiped tears from his eyes. Many northerners, although they disagreed with Brown's raid, began to admire his courage. Locked in a cell, Brown accomplished with his pen what he could not do with guns and pikes.

On the morning of December 2, 1859, Brown left his cell for the last time. Surrounded by guards and a crowd of thousands, Brown rode in a wagon to the site of his execution. Calmly he mounted the gallows and waited as the noose of the rope was tightened around his neck. According to one observer, Brown stood "as motionless as a statue." A hush fell over the crowd. The order was given for the platform to be

This picture, perhaps the most famous photograph of John Brown, convinced people that Brown was a madman who deserved punishment for his raid on Harpers Ferry.

released and within a few minutes, Brown was dead. His body was returned to North Elba, New York, for burial.

Abolitionists throughout the North hailed Brown as a hero of liberty and freedom. In Albany, New York, a one hundred-gun salute was fired in his honor.

John Brown ascends the gallows in preparation to be hanged.

The northern reaction to Brown's death angered the South. For almost thirty years, southerners had endured harsh criticism of slavery. Each year, antislavery forces seemed to grow stronger. John Brown's raid was the final blow. To many southerners, Brown represented the North's desire to destroy the South. To protect their way of life, many southerners began to believe that they must leave the Union. John Brown's raid had forced the North and the South to the breaking point. The Charleston [South Carolina] *Mercury* wrote, "there is no peace for the South in the Union. The South must control her own destinies or perish."

Brown's prediction that his raid would cause civil war came true within a year of his death. In November 1860, Abraham Lincoln was elected president. Soon after, the southern states, led by South Carolina, left the Union and the American Civil War began. Although Brown was dead, his raid at Harpers Ferry was not forgotten. As Union soldiers marched off to fight the South they sang: "John Brown's body lies a-moldering in the grave, but his soul goes marching on."

In 1863, Lincoln signed the Emancipation Proclamation—a document that freed all of the slaves in the rebelling states. In 1865, the South surrendered and the Thirteenth Amendment to the Constitution was passed, banning slavery forever. John Brown's dream at last had come true.

President
Abraham Lincoln

Today, some people consider Brown a madman who violently attacked and killed innocent people. Others believe he is a hero who fought for equality and freedom. Whatever is said or written about him, John Brown struggled through years of hardship and disappointment for the cause he believed in. Finally, when he had nothing else to give, Brown sacrificed his life. In death, Brown accomplished what he could not do while he was alive. His raid helped break up the Union and bring about the destruction of slavery.

A picket fence surrounds John Brown's grave in North Elba, New York.

GLOSSARY

abolitionist – person who worked to outlaw slavery before the Civil War

armory – place where weapons are stored

arsenal – place where weapons and ammunition are made or stored

bayonet – long knife that can be fastened to the end of a rifle

Congress – the part of the United States government that is responsible for making laws, it is made up of the Senate and the House of Representatives

engine house

engine house – place where fire engines are kept and serviced

gallows – wooden frame used to hang criminals

immoral – unfair, without a sense of what is right and what is wrong

militia – group of citizens who are trained to fight but who only serve in time of emergency

militia

plantation – large farm that usually specializes in growing one crop

raid – sudden, surprise attack

rebellion – armed fight, any struggle against the people in charge of something

sack – to steal things from a place that has been captured in a war or battle

treason – the crime of attempting to overthrow the government of your own country, of spying for another country, or helping an enemy during a war

truce – temporary agreement to stop fighting

TIMELINE

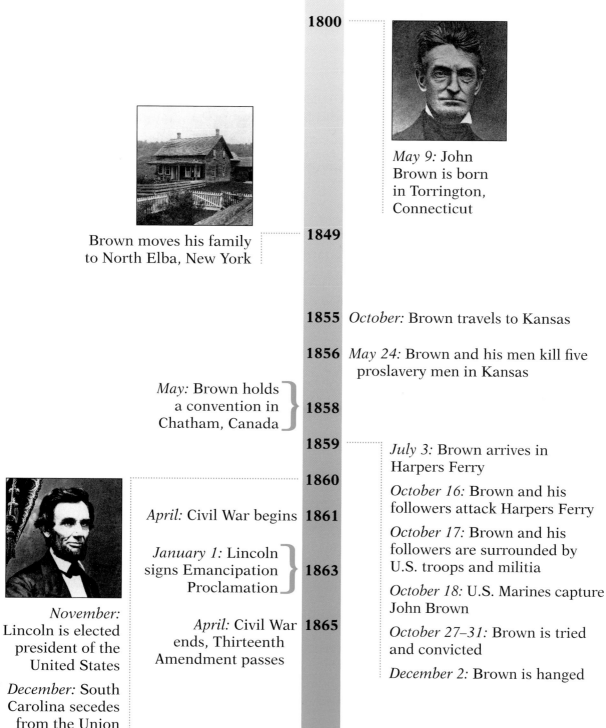

1800

May 9: John Brown is born in Torrington, Connecticut

Brown moves his family to North Elba, New York

1849

1855 *October:* Brown travels to Kansas

1856 *May 24:* Brown and his men kill five proslavery men in Kansas

May: Brown holds a convention in Chatham, Canada } **1858**

1859 *July 3:* Brown arrives in Harpers Ferry

1860 *October 16:* Brown and his followers attack Harpers Ferry

April: Civil War begins **1861** *October 17:* Brown and his followers are surrounded by U.S. troops and militia

January 1: Lincoln signs Emancipation Proclamation } **1863** *October 18:* U.S. Marines capture John Brown

October 27–31: Brown is tried and convicted

April: Civil War ends, Thirteenth Amendment passes **1865** *December 2:* Brown is hanged

November: Lincoln is elected president of the United States

December: South Carolina secedes from the Union

INDEX (*Boldface* page numbers indicate illustrations.)

PHOTO CREDITS

Photographs ©: AP/Wide World Photos: 17 center; Collection of the Boston Athenaeum: 26;
Corbis-Bettmann: 11 (Lee Snider), 5 bottom (UPI), 4, 14, 21 bottom, 23, 27, 28, 29, 31 bottom left;
Harpers Ferry Historical Association: 9, 10, 20 bottom, 30 top; Kansas State Historical Society,
Topeka: 3, 17 bottom, 21 top, 31 right; Library of Congress: 6, 18, 19, 20 top, 31 top left; North Wind
Picture Archives: 1, 5 top; Stock Montage, Inc.: cover, 2, 16, 17 top, 22, 24, 30 bottom. Maps by
TJS Design, Inc.

PICTURE IDENTIFICATIONS

Cover: John Brown; Title Page: John Brown's "fort" in Harpers Ferry, Virginia; Page 2: The last
moments of John Brown's life

ABOUT THE AUTHOR

Brendan January was born and raised in Pleasantville, New York. He earned his B.A. in history and
English at Haverford College and an M.A. in Journalism from Columbia University. An American
history enthusiast, he has written several books for Children's Press, including *The Emancipation
Proclamation, Fort Sumter, The Dred Scott Decision, The Lincoln-Douglas Debates, The Assassination
of Abraham Lincoln,* and *Reconstruction* (Cornerstones of Freedom). Mr. January is a newspaper
reporter and lives in New Jersey.